PENGUIN BOOKS

YOU DON'T NEED TO SMACK

Glen Stenhouse has been a child and educational psychologist
for more than 25 years. He has extensive experience with all
types of children's behavioural, emotional, developmental and
learning problems, from toddlers to teenagers. He is also a
specialist report writer for the Family Court. Glen is the author
of *Children's Nightmares*, *Confident Children* and *Practical Parenting*.
He is in private practice in Auckland.

YOU DON'T NEED TO SMACK

Simple strategies for dealing with misbehaviour
GLEN STENHOUSE

PENGUIN BOOKS

Published by the Penguin Group

Penguin Group (NZ), 67 Apollo Drive, Rosedale
North Shore 0632, New Zealand (a division of Pearson New Zealand Ltd)
Penguin Group (USA) Inc., 375 Hudson Street,
New York, New York 10014, USA
Penguin Group (Canada), 90 Eglinton Avenue East, Suite 700, Toronto,
Ontario, M4P 2Y3, Canada (a division of Pearson Penguin Canada Inc.)
Penguin Books Ltd, 80 Strand, London, WC2R 0RL, England
Penguin Ireland, 25 St Stephen's Green,
Dublin 2, Ireland (a division of Penguin Books Ltd)
Penguin Group (Australia), 250 Camberwell Road, Camberwell,
Victoria 3124, Australia (a division of Pearson Australia Group Pty Ltd)
Penguin Books India Pvt Ltd, 11, Community Centre,
Panchsheel Park, New Delhi – 110 017, India
Penguin Books (South Africa) (Pty) Ltd, 24 Sturdee Avenue,
Rosebank, Johannesburg 2196, South Africa

Penguin Books Ltd, Registered Offices: 80 Strand, London, WC2R 0RL, England

First published by Penguin Group (NZ), 2008
1 3 5 7 9 10 8 6 4 2

Copyright © Glen Stenhouse, 2008

The right of Glen Stenhouse to be identified as the author of this work in terms of
section 96 of the Copyright Act 1994 is hereby asserted.

Designed by Daniel Mesnage
Illustration by Anna Egan-Reid
Typeset by Pindar New Zealand (Egan Reid)
Printed in Australia by McPherson's Printing Group

ISBN 978 014 300867 5

A catalogue record for this book is available
from the National Library of New Zealand.

www.penguin.co.nz

Contents

Foreword

I predict that parents who sit down with *You Don't Need to Smack* will feel themselves start to relax. Glen Stenhouse's writing 'voice' is warm, sensible and reassuring, just what parents need as they navigate the maze of competing parenting philosophies.

I have known Glen for many years as a psychologist and as a writer of information for parents. His kind, calm, witty style conveys parenting wisdom distilled from vast experience of real life with real New Zealand families.

'Parenting is not complicated. Hard work, yes. Complicated, no.'

He distills what is needed to be a good parent. That six-bullet-point list on page 24 should be engraved in stone and placed in every school, maternity hospital and sports club. We all need reminding that parents need to be attentive, thoughtful, sensitive, 'self-sacrificing to a remarkable degree', patient and prepared to give their time generously.

Glen warns his readers that this is not a politically correct book. For example, he thinks parents should operate a benign dictatorship and gives them some guidelines in doing it, allowing for challenges such as temperamental difference. His focus on prevention by giving appropriate time and attention to the child is balanced with non-violent means of dealing with children's infringements of parental rules and values.

He has particularly valuable advice for 'older, conscientious parents', who 'try to fill their children's lives with every opportunity and learning experience possible, particularly in the toddler and preschool years, rather than just letting them play and be children'.

As someone who has been concerned with and about New Zealand parenting behaviour for 20 years, I can only wish that every new parent will have this book beside their bed as a friendly and reassuring guide in their most important career.

Lesley Max
CEO Great Potentials
Chair, Parenting Council of New Zealand

CHAPTER 1

About this book

This book is written for parents who don't want to smack their children – which is every parent I've ever met. Some parents think that smacking is the right thing to do; some parents think they sometimes have no choice other than to use physical punishment, but no parent I have ever met actually *wants* to smack.

For more than twenty-five years a major part of my work has been helping parents manage the difficult behaviour of their children. One of the things I have learned is that the vast majority of children *do not need* to be smacked to keep them in line. Secondly, for really difficult children where you might think there is no alternative, *smacking doesn't work*. These are generally the children who laugh at you when you smack them, say it doesn't hurt or try to hit you back.

So, the evidence is clear to me that smacking as a behaviour-management tool is unnecessary for the vast majority of children and ineffective for the rest. However, there are some simple, commonsense strategies you can use that will enable you to manage your children's behaviour really well without smacking. That's what this book is about. Its focus is managing the behaviour of children from preschool to early adolescence, concentrating mainly on the primary school years.

I should warn you that this is not a politically correct book. I use plain, everyday language like 'good', 'bad', 'right', 'wrong' and 'naughty'. I talk about strategies for managing children's behaviour, which might sound manipulative and controlling to some. I also talk about the need for punishment. If words or concepts like this offend you, put this book down right now.

In the following pages I make the point more than once that parenting is not complicated. It is hard work, but not complicated. The number of books written about parenting seems to imply that it is a technical, specialised subject full of traps for the uninformed, and that it should not be undertaken without lots of reading. I disagree.

Parenting needs very little specialist knowledge. What it does need is commitment, energy, patience, perseverance and common sense, all motivated by love. And the love comes naturally.

If you are looking for something surprising or revolutionary in this book, you'll be disappointed. As I often say to the parents who come to see me, in the parenting business there is nothing new under the sun. Instead, what I have to say is simple, practical and down to earth. Almost all of it is based on experience rather than theory. The suggestions I make have been tested with thousands of families and, if you are prepared to put in a little bit of effort, you will find that they work.

CHAPTER 2

Why smack?

I define smacking as hitting a child with an open hand on the leg, bottom or hand for the purpose of controlling their behaviour.

Why do we do it? Why is it such a common practice among parents? Well, almost always, we smack our children because they have done something particularly naughty, to make them stop doing something they shouldn't be doing, or to make them do something they don't want to do. Like all of us, children want to do their own thing in their own way in their own time, but of course they can't always do that. We are responsible for our children's behaviour, and what we want to do is shape them into civilised little people who can be part of a happily functioning family and, eventually, responsible members of our society.

Almost always we are able to mould and influence our children's behaviour into acceptable patterns without the threat or use of physical force, but sometimes we feel we have no other option. This is usually due to two situations. The first is a *heat-of-the-moment* scenario, where the combination of naughty behaviour and our stress or impatience leads to an impulsive smack. The second is the *painted-ourselves-into-a-corner* scenario, where we threaten to smack unless our child complies with a directive. The situation is not particularly heated. The child refuses to comply. We then feel that to maintain our credibility, we have to carry through our threat.

It is more difficult to avoid smacking in heated situations than in the *you-give-me-no-option* type, but it can be done, and we will talk more about that later.

In the meantime, if you have been smacking your child, it does not mean that you are a bad person. It does not mean that you will turn your child into a mental-health statistic in later years. It does not mean that you have irreparably damaged your relationship with your child. Smacking is, and has been for a very long time, a common method of controlling children's behaviour. Most of us will have been smacked ourselves as children, and this did not stop us from loving our parents, nor did it turn us into aggressive psychopaths.

But we don't *want* to smack our children. We regret it after we have done so, and we wish that there was an alternative. What I am saying in this book is that there *are* other options. They take more planning, effort and perseverance than smacking, but they are also more effective in the long run.

CHAPTER 3

Punishment

Most children's behaviour can be managed most of the time by using positive techniques, but because almost all children have a bit of mischief in them they sometimes need the application of an *unpleasant consequence* to keep them on the right track.

In the context of child-rearing, that's what punishment is: the use of an unpleasant consequence to help children decide to do the right thing. It's pretty much like the use of fines and imprisonment to help adults decide not to break the law. Most people would probably comply with the law even if we didn't have penalties, but we do need penalties for those who sometimes choose not to.

It's the same with children. The majority of children past toddlerhood are compliant and co-operative most of the time, and there are even some little angels who hardly ever stray onto the dark side, but most children will occasionally need to have their behaviour realigned. When positive and preventive strategies haven't worked, this may mean that you will have to use a penalty or punishment.

These days the word 'punishment' is often avoided in discussions about child-rearing, as if it carries implications of harsh treatment and abuse. Far from it. Punishment is a useful and necessary word when talking about the management of children's behaviour. The term 'discipline' is often used today in the place of punishment but to me that word carries quite a different meaning. The way I see it, discipline is an aspect or quality of *character* that children should have as the result of being well brought-up. I think of discipline as the ability to manage and regulate our own behaviour according to a code or set of values, and this is certainly an aim we should have for our children. If they are eventually able to control their own behaviour according to principles we have taught them, we will have done our job well.

So, we should not shrink from using the plain and simple word 'punishment', or 'penalty' if you prefer. It is a normal, essential component of managing most children's behaviour. It should only be a minor part of any behaviour-management plan, but it is very unlikely we will be able to get by without it completely. We will talk more later about the types of penalties available to us.

CHAPTER 4

Parenting is simple

Parenting is not complicated. Hard work, yes. Complicated, no.

If you judged by the number of books about parenting, you might think that you needed a university degree to do it, but thankfully that's not the case. We psychologists have somehow managed to create the impression that parenting is a technical and tricky business, but the fact is that the results of much psychological research into child-rearing are simply the confirmation of common sense.

Psychology is different from other sciences such as chemistry and biology, because we all have access to the raw data of what psychology is about. We experience it inside our own heads all the time, and we are constantly exposed to the behaviour of other people. From our constant immersion in this sea of information about how people think, feel and behave, most of us develop a pretty good practical guidebook about how and why people feel and behave the way they do. This guidebook works quite well most of the time, even though there are obviously some behaviours – our own and others' – that we can't understand or explain.

This home-made instruction book for understanding everyday human behaviour also works pretty well with our own children, because children aren't complicated to work out either. Their needs are very simple, as follows:

- to feel loved;
- to feel safe;
- to have generous doses of your time and attention;
- to be fed, clothed, and housed;
- to be able to explore and learn about their world;
- to play;
- to develop their abilities and interests; and
- to have friends.

That's pretty much it! Parenting is increasingly being made to appear to be a very difficult job, which carries huge responsibility and has calamitous consequences for our children if we get it wrong. As a result, conscientious parents start to worry about their parenting; worry about whether they are getting it 'right', worry about whether they even know what 'right' is, worry that somehow they might inadvertently ruin their children's lives.

In fact, parenting is simple. To be a good parent you need to be:

- attentive to your children's needs;
- thoughtful about how best to provide for their needs;
- sensitive to how they change as they grow and develop;
- self-sacrificing to a remarkable degree;
- patient; and
- prepared to give your time generously.

That's not complicated, is it? And the fact is that it all comes naturally. I didn't even mention the need to love your child, because that is an automatic reflex to the presence of your children in your life. You can't help but love them. And once you love them, the other aspects of parenting will come pretty much automatically.

One more point. For loving parents there is a wide margin of error in bringing up children because they are amazingly adaptable and resilient. Trust your common sense and the parenting instincts that evolution has given you. You won't go too far wrong.

CHAPTER 5

Ages and stages

Children of different ages need different approaches to their behaviour management.

To start right at the beginning, obviously babies don't need behaviour management. They need us to be attentive and responsive to their requirements. They need to eat, sleep, be kept warm and clean, interact with us, begin to interact with their environment and learn the routines of how all these things happen. They just need lots of looking after.

Believe it or not, babies come in different brands. Some are happy, placid and easy to please. Some are quiet observers. Some can't wait to engage with the world. Some are grizzly, hard to soothe, cry a lot and don't sleep much. The grumpy ones can make you feel very frustrated and angry at times but, other than trying a programme to teach them to settle by themselves and sleep through the night, you just have to do the best you can to meet their needs.

However, you should seek your doctor's advice if your baby is chronically unhappy or you feel that you aren't coping.

Once children start to walk and talk, the real business of shaping and training begins. Toddlers are even more time-intensive than babies because they sleep less and are now mobile. There is literally no escape from this fact of life. When they are awake, toddlers need someone to be with them constantly, watching them, meeting their physical needs, playing with them and keeping them safe. If toddlers are monitored, looked after, played with and protected from environmental dangers, they will need very little in the way of direct behaviour management. The very busy ones are exhausting, but if you keep them occupied things should go well most of the time.

It goes without saying that babies can't be naughty. Toddlers can be wilful and determined but not really naughty; not in the sense of deliberately doing things they know they shouldn't.

The best strategies to get toddlers out of troublesome situations are *distraction* and *re-direction*. You can divert most toddlers' attention from whatever it is you don't want them to do by offering a more attractive alternative. Any protest tends to be short-lived. Persevere and the storm will pass. Smacking isn't necessary.

Strategies for the next stages in development – preschool and school-age children – are what this book is mainly about, because these are the ages at which parents are most likely to use smacking as a behaviour-management tool.

Teenagers can definitely be naughty, but they are beyond the scope of this book. In the teenage years you are drawing on all the hard work you will have done in the earlier years, particularly with an emphasis on values, mutual respect, trust and encouragement to independence. There will be much more discussion and negotiation than there needs to be with younger children, and you have to change your parenting style gradually to accommodate their growing wish to be self-reliant. But let's not look too far ahead. Let's concentrate first on getting the early years right.

CHAPTER 6

Time and attention

Now we get down to the details of how to manage your child's behaviour without the use of smacking.

There are two main parts to our discussion. The first, and by far the biggest, part is *prevention*. There are many things you can do to reduce the probability of being in a situation with your child where you feel you need to smack.

The second and much smaller part of the book deals with *punishments* or *penalties*, which are alternatives to smacking. This section is brief because there aren't many of them.

The first preventive strategy is giving your time and attention to your child. This is essential and unavoidable in the first few years, because of the child's dependency and need for adult input at this stage of life. As children grow older their care is less time-intensive, but your input and involvement is obviously still very important for a whole range of reasons.

In the context of this book, one of the reasons you need to give your children your time and attention is because during the time you spend together you build enduring qualities in your relationship such as love, trust, respect and an intimate knowledge of each other.

In the early years, your time with your child is largely responsive to her immediate physical needs. Then come the toddler years with the need to be able to explore the world safely and develop physical skills. In the preschool years come increasing independence, the development of a wide range of indoor and outdoor play skills, and the skills of social play. During all this time your child needs your reassuring presence and involvement, partly as a secure base and haven for exploring her environment; partly as a source of comfort, reassurance and encouragement; and partly as protector, guide and instructor. As your child learns to trust you as a loving, protecting, and reassuring presence in her life, you are building a basis of power and influence with her, because she will naturally want to please you, not upset or anger you, as she gets older. Even very young children can be sensitive to negative moods in their parents, and may try to comfort them if they appear sad or upset.

Let me be very clear about one thing here. Even though it may sound like it, I am definitely *not* suggesting that you should develop a strong relationship with your child so that you can use it in a purely practical and calculated way to make your job easier as a parent. For a start, the love your child feels for you, and vice versa, comes automatically, so it doesn't have to be artificially cultivated. But it is a fact that a loving, dedicated relationship with your children will bear dividends in behaviour management because they will not want to hurt or upset someone who is important to them. Of course that is not going to be enough to prevent unacceptable behaviour from occurring, but for most children it will influence their behaviour at those times when they are making a choice about whether or not to follow your rules.

CHAPTER 7

Routines and rules

No family can function effectively without routines and rules. In fact, a good definition of a dysfunctional family is one *without* routines and rules, where everyone does pretty much what they want, when they want, without values or boundaries. They are families without structure. Their members figure heavily in crime statistics and the news headlines for child abuse.

But I know your family isn't like this because you picked up this book! You are interested in doing a good job as a parent. You love your children and want to do the best you can for them. It's a good bet that you have values that are important to you, and values are the basis of good rules.

Usually our values aren't explicit. Unless you are an active church member or belong to a political group, you probably don't think about your values very much. Most of us don't. We take them for granted. But if you want to be an effective parent, it's worth putting a little time, thought and discussion into this issue. Ask yourself:

- What do I really believe in?
- What's important to me?
- When I get down to the bottom line, what am I living and working for?
- How do I want my children to turn out?
- What sort of adults do I want them to be?
- I will be proud of them if they do . . . what?

Parents who come to me to talk about their children's problems often say that they just want their children to be happy. That's a goal we would all agree with, but is that enough? Most of us would also add that we want our children to be healthy, to have fun, to do as well as they can at school, to have friends, learn a sport or cultural activity of some kind and to be kind and considerate to others. And I suppose if they achieve all that, then they will be happy.

Another goal I think is particularly important for children is that they become independent of us, and will eventually be able to function confidently in the world as self-sufficient, self-reliant adults. I will talk more about this later.

But all these long-term goals are achieved by taking little steps every day. Each day brings the opportunity for children to move along the road to being healthy, happy, independent and considerate young people. And who is their guide and tutor in all this? You guessed it.

We naturally guide, prompt, encourage and remind our children about how to do things, what not to do and how to behave appropriately in certain situations. Some of these things are trivial, such as putting the lid back on the peanut butter jar when you've finished with it, and others are important, such as telling the truth and not hurting people. Whatever the rule is, be explicit about it:

- Put things away when you've finished with them.
- Say 'please' and 'thank you'.
- Don't be cheeky.
- Take turns when you're playing a game.

- Let your visitor choose what game they want to play.
- Do your homework before you go out to play.
- Do your chores.

When parents are having problems with their children's behaviour, one of the first things I suggest is that they make sure that everyone is clear about what the house rules are. If the rules are vague or inconsistently applied then you can't blame your child for trying to take advantage of that.

I suggest that parents take the trouble to sit down with their children, if they are of school age, and talk about the rules needed to make your household tick along smoothly. Write them down and put them up somewhere where everyone can see them. Then when your child is doing something inappropriate, you can ask:

'What are you doing?'

'Playing on the PlayStation.'

'What's the rule about that?'

'No screen-time till homework is done.'

Parental pause.
Parental look.
'Okay, okay, I'm going.'
'Thank you.'

Asking your child what they are doing when they are up to something inappropriate is a good technique. This gives them the opportunity to think about the situation and choose to do the right thing instead of getting straight into a confrontation. Referring to a rule is better than simply saying, 'Because I said so!' (Although there will be times when you will need to say this, and that's fine.) It is better if authority resides in the family rules, especially if they have been agreed to by everyone, than simply in you as a parent (although, as I say, there is a necessary place for that too).

Just being clear about your house rules and having them written down can have a positive effect on children's behaviour.

Having *clear routines* for the basic activities of the day is also very helpful in avoiding unnecessary arguments about whether or how certain things should be done. If you have standard routines for getting ready for school, meal-times, bathtime, bedtime and so on, there is less scope for disputatious little persons to try to change the system according to their whim or preference of the moment. If things are never the same from one day to the next, then children will at times try to use this uncertainty to push their own agenda.

One last point: in the interest of fairness, justice and your credibility as a parent, remember that rules apply as much to grown-ups as to children.

CHAPTER 8

Act with confidence

The huge amount of discussion in the media about parenting and the large number of parenting books on the shelves of bookshops have tended to make today's conscientious parents uncertain about how to raise and manage their children.

That's a pity, partly because it's quite unnecessary and partly because uncertainty will undermine your confidence. If your confidence is undermined you are less likely to parent with decisiveness and authority. When that happens, any child worth their Weet-Bix will try to take advantage of the situation by promoting their own agenda with determination and enthusiasm.

Let us not be starry-eyed and romantic about this parenting business. As wonderful as children are, they tend to be selfish little creatures at heart (as we all do) and want what they want. Our job is to give them what they need. This often involves a clash of wills and, to speak plainly, it is important that we emerge from these clashes as the winner.

A lot of what happens in families is about power, but I'm not going to go into that big topic here, other than to say that children want their share of power and control too. Of course they need some say about what happens in their lives, but not on matters where you as their parent have the right and responsibility to make executive decisions in their best interests.

The key point here is that when you must ask or direct your child to do something, or to stop doing something, act with authority. This doesn't mean you need to raise your voice; in fact it's better if you don't. Just think back to your school days. Which teachers did you respect more – the ones who yelled and shouted or the ones who spoke quietly but firmly? Exactly. So be the same. When you are giving your child an instruction, be firm and decisive in how you say it. Be polite but keep it brief. This greatly increases the chance of compliance.

If you ask hesitantly, you increase the probability that your child will argue the point. And, for heaven's sake, don't *ask* your child if they would like to have a bath now, or would like to go to bed now. And don't end every request or directive with 'Okay?' Adding the tag 'Okay?' is an invitation to children to decline, or argue with, your request. For families to function, certain things have to get done every day, and children have to be told to do things. If you ask children if they would *like* to do something that doesn't involve screens or chocolate, what do you think they will say?

Act with confidence in your parenting because you are the *world expert* in your children. You have good, intuitive judgement about what's best for them. Trust that judgement and parent with confidence. If you do that, you will make it much more likely that your children will do as you say.

CHAPTER 9

Show confidence

In the previous chapter I stressed how important it is that we act with confidence as parents. In addition to this, it is also important to *show* confidence in our children.

If we make it clear to them that we trust them to be good, that we have confidence in their ability to make the right choice and that we know they can act responsibly, then we are helping them to see themselves and think of themselves in that way. If they have a self-image of being good, responsible and sensible, then they are more likely to *behave* that way. Why? Because *not* behaving that way – not making the right choices, not being responsible – will clash with their self-image and will make them feel uncomfortable.

We want our children to be good, sensible, considerate and responsible. An important part of that process is for them to think of themselves in this way, so they will act in accordance with that self-image.

So, when your child does something good, point it out to him: 'I am so proud of you. What you did was a very considerate thing to do. You are becoming a very thoughtful boy.' Don't gush. Just be factual and say briefly how you feel about it. Make occasional comments like: 'You are a sensible boy. I know I can trust you to do the right thing.' Try to be specific about the quality you want to encourage, rather than just saying, 'What a good boy!' By highlighting your child's good traits in this simple and matter-of-fact way you are fostering the development of those traits much more effectively than by focusing on failings.

CHAPTER 10

Less discussion

Here's a problem. Firstly, there is no doubt that good parents talk with their children a lot, explain things, answer their questions and discuss things with them. By doing this we increase children's understanding of the world, help them to develop their reasoning skills, teach them that discussion is the best way to sort out problems and also show them respect by involving them and listening to them. This is obviously a much better approach than the old one of 'Be quiet and do as you're told'.

However, I think things have gone too far. Today's conscientious parents have taken on board the message that it's good to talk about things with your children, but that doesn't mean *everything* is up for negotiation and that *everything* needs to be discussed and explained in detail. Neither does it mean that children, especially young children, should have input into *everything* that goes on.

It's important to remember that families are not democracies, where everyone has equal influence and an equal vote. The fact is that families are benign dictatorships and *you* are in charge. The big guys call the shots. Of course children need to have their say (try to stop them) but they are not equal partners in the family business.

There is a time and place for discussion; for example, at family meetings. Once children reach school age, family meetings are a good idea. They give everyone a chance to talk about the issues that are bothering them, to learn good listening skills, to learn about solving problems through discussion and to show respect for each other's opinions. But the decision-making power remains with parents. Listening is good, discussion is good, but the day-to-day functioning of the family often needs children to just do as they are told. Do not feel bad about this. It is okay to be directive. It is okay to say 'Thou shalt' and 'Thou shalt not'.

Some children are a lot more assertive and argumentative than others. They, in particular, need you to be decisive and direct because they will use the combined skills of a used car salesman, a criminal barrister and a football player annoyed at the ref's decision to convince you to see things their way. Discussing things with children like this is playing right into their hands: they will either win the argument or drive you to behave in ways you will later feel embarrassed about.

Some discussion is good, but not bargaining, pleading, persuading, cajoling or negotiating. In today's schools children are taught to discuss, reason, justify their positions and explain their viewpoints. By implication, there are no absolute positions, no right and wrong, just good arguments and not-so-good arguments. Discussion is everything, not the outcome. It doesn't matter much what you think as long as you can justify it with evidence and reasoning.

This approach should definitely not be transferred to home as a method of resolving issues, although children will try to do so. In your home there *is* right and wrong, there *are* absolute positions and there *are* rules. Sometimes there will be a need to talk about these things, and to maybe modify them according to changing circumstances, but not at the point of action. Not at the time when you are getting ready to go to work and school. Not when things need to get done.

It is important that school-age and older children feel they are listened to, but the time for listening is not in the heat of the moment. Make it clear that you are always prepared to talk about things, but at the right time, when you are able to sit down and can each explain and discuss your points of view.

CHAPTER 11

Don't ask ten times

This is such a simple one. Presumably, when you ask your child to do something or to stop doing something, you mean it, and you want it to happen. Usually, you want it to happen now, or very soon. So why ask your child several times with no visible result?

Here's the drill:

- Think about what you are asking your child to do. Is it a fair request and does it need to happen?
- If the answer is yes, first *go to where your child is, get her attention*, then tell her clearly what you want.
- If nothing happens, say, 'What did I ask you to do?'
- If nothing happens, stop what you are doing, go back to your child and say, 'Come on, I asked you to do X. Let's get started.' Then stop talking and make sure that your child complies.

If you get into the habit of asking your children ten times before you get serious, you can bet they will ignore you the first nine times. So ask *once*, give *one* reminder at the most, then *take action*. By 'take action' I mean using your physical presence and physical prompts if necessary to make things happen.

To be a credible, effective, respected parent, mean what you say and carry through on it.

For challenging children who tend to be non-compliant, this drill is particularly important. The first step of asking yourself whether your request is necessary becomes even more critical, because once you've asked *you can't back down*. Ever. With chronically difficult children, when you ask that first question, 'Is this a fair and necessary request?' you are effectively asking, 'Is this worth a tussle?' Sometimes the answer may be no, and that's the end of that. If the answer is yes, you have started on a process that must end in their compliance.

One last thing: don't forget a word of thanks or acknowledgement when the request has been carried out.

CHAPTER 12

No means no

Like all of us, children want the world to go their way. Sometimes they can be very powerful in advocating for their viewpoint. You must be *more* powerful. Think *RoboCop*.

The little word 'No', is a symbol of your authority as a parent. The word 'Yes' is unlikely ever to cause a problem, but 'No' can produce much wailing and gnashing of teeth. It can unleash a tidal wave of fury against you, but you must stand firm.

'No' does not mean, 'This is when the negotiations begin.' It does not mean, 'You are now invited to present forcefully your strongest arguments against me, and we'll see where we end up.' It means, 'End of story.'

If you have said no and your child protests, tell them that you are not going to discuss the matter, then *say no more*. Do not respond. Walk away if you have to.

If you do respond, the situation becomes like a game

of tennis. Your child fires a ball at you, you hit it back, he volleys it, you give it your best back-hand and so on. Do not play this game. Put down your racket and walk off the court.

The amount of effort your children put into trying to persuade you to change your mind is related to their expectation that you will cave in. The greater the chance that you will say, 'Oh for heaven's sake, do what you like!' the greater the chance they will keep hammering on.

If you have been in the habit of giving in to pressure tactics and decide that you are now going to be a rock, it will almost certainly take a while for the message to get through to your child that things have changed. During this period, he is likely to do even more of what has worked in the past, which can be difficult to resist. However, be assured that if you hang in there, the intensity of the protests will drop off. Sometimes it can happen quite quickly, but I promise nothing.

So, when your child asks you for something, unless it is a minor issue *think* for a few seconds before you reply, because once you have said no there is no turning back. If you feel you need more time before making a decision, just say so: 'I need to think about that for a bit. I'll tell you this afternoon.' But keep your word. Many a child has told me the sad tale of parents saying, 'I'll think about it,' then never getting back to them. Not good for your credibility or their trust.

CHAPTER 13

Talk less, act more

If there is one factor that, in my experience, tends to be associated with less effective parenting, it is talking too much.

We have already looked at the role of discussion and explanation in child-rearing, and these things are good and important in their place.

But it seems that conscientious parents now think every action and instruction needs to be wrapped in a package of explanation and justification, as if they are pleading a case in court.

One simple point: the more you talk, the less your child will listen. If it's just a chat about a movie or a discussion about why the sky is blue, that's fine. Go for it. But if you want to tell her why she shouldn't do something, keep the explanation simple: 'Don't pull the cat's tail. It will hurt her.' Don't give lengthy, tedious sermons after she's been busted for a misdemeanour, just something like: 'I'm disappointed in you. You know what the rule is about telling the truth. I hope it doesn't happen again.' (Plus a penalty, if you decide to impose it: see Chapter 26 on the three strikes system.)

We all know that the longer the sermon, the less effective it is. So keep 'em brief. This is particularly the case with children who are frequent offenders. They have heard everything you can tell them a thousand times already, so why do it? You may think that you are somehow being a good parent by moralising at length after the event, but believe me you are wasting your time. Get to the point, impose the punishment, then move on.

One particularly useless question to ask is, 'Why did you do it?' For a response you will either get staring at the shoes, a mumble, a plausible lie or blaming an innocent bystander, when the real answer is something like: 'I just wanted to.' There is *never* a good reason for doing bad stuff, so why ask?

Good parenting is more about actions than words. It is

about what you do for and with your child, and much less about what you say. This is particularly the case in the area of dealing with misdeeds.

CHAPTER 14

Ignoring

Ignoring is a very powerful way of dealing with some undesirable behaviours. As odd as it may sound, in some situations the best response is *no* response.

It's important to understand here that ignoring means exactly that: making no response. Acting as if nothing has happened. Acting as if your child is not there. Human beings are social creatures, and to be ignored by others, especially those who are emotionally important to you, has a big impact.

Parents sometimes tell me that they have been told to ignore all bad behaviour. This is not good advice. Some behaviours cannot be ignored, in particular *aggression*, *deliberate destruction*, and *defiance*. They cannot be ignored because it is like giving your child tacit permission to behave that way, or giving the message that you are powerless to deal with them. We will talk later about how to respond to these behaviours (see Chapter 27 on time-out).

Ignoring is for minor misbehaviour that has *minimal or no impact* on anybody other than the child, or on their environment. Examples are sulking, minor tantrums, silliness, attention-seeking, showing off and mild cheekiness. I would also include bad language in this category, but you have to be pretty staunch to carry it off. I think that the best response when children use bad language is *not* to respond. To act as if nothing was said. Bad language is only ever used for effect, and if there is no effect it will soon fizzle out. The problem with ignoring it is that if someone else is present when it happens, such as a friend or – even worse – your mother, you feel obliged to do something. But ignoring is the best policy in the long run. If necessary, briefly explain to bystanders what you're doing and stick to your guns. Even gruesome swearing from teenagers is best dealt with in this way.

Remember that ignoring does not mean to give minimal attention, to make some brief comment or even to say, 'I am not paying attention to you while you behave like that.' It means to make no response at all. Don't make eye contact. Carry on with what you are doing, If necessary, walk away.

Ignoring is a particularly helpful strategy with children who tend to be difficult much of the time. With a child like this, if you pick up on every little act of misbehaviour, your life will be one long battle. Ignoring minor misbehaviour is a way of reducing the number of fights in the day and conserving your energy, as well as being an effective tactic. It works because most children really don't like to be ignored.

One important point: you must be as consistent as possible in the behaviours you ignore. If you ignore a certain behaviour on Monday then come out blazing about it on Tuesday, you will greatly undermine the effectiveness of the strategy.

This consistency rule applies to all your behaviour-management strategies. By consistency, I mean 'as consistent as humanly possible'. Nobody is ever 100% consistent, but do aim high.

Before you implement your ignoring policy, think about which behaviours you will apply it to, then tell your children about it. If you tell your children which behaviours you will ignore then they don't have to spend time trying to work out if maybe you didn't notice what they did, whether you really are ignoring them and whether it's worth trying you on. Having a transparent policy on such behaviour strategies as ignoring makes it more likely that each incident will be resolved more quickly, because children know what the drill is. This is particularly so if children also know you mean what you say.

One last point: if ignoring doesn't stop the behaviour after a reasonable amount of time, or it escalates to the point that you *can't* ignore it any more (in other words, it is having an impact on somebody or something) then use a punishment (see chapters 26 and 27 on three strikes and time-out).

CHAPTER 15

Keep 'em busy

One of the best preventives for misbehaviour is keeping children busy with productive, positive, fun activities.

In some ways this is easier for parents today than it was in the old days, because of all the entertainment that's now available for children, but in other ways it's harder.

In my generation, children of school age could confidently be left to play by themselves. You would easily find things to do, sometimes around the house, usually outside in the yard, and quite often by wandering over the road to a friend's house. Then the two of you would meander down the road to see what your other mates were up to. Before you knew it, it was lunchtime or dinnertime, and you'd wander home. Or the neighbours would feed you. Parents didn't ever seem to worry about what their children were up to, partly because you could probably hear the neighbourhood gang playing cricket a few doors away. Or racing their bikes. Or playing cops and robbers.

Also, children tended to go round in pairs or small groups so that safety wasn't a big issue. And there weren't many cars.

In those days there were no screens to watch, and very few toys compared to the deluge of baubles that engulf today's children. So you made your own fun with whatever came to hand. Bits of wood. Making huts. Making roads for your cars in the dirt. Just exploring. Nobody had ever heard of 'play-dates'. The very idea would have seemed bizarre.

Anyway, enough reminiscing. We all know things have changed. Backyards have all but gone and children can't be left to wander around the neighbourhood on their own any more. Their bedrooms are knee-high in toys and there are screens everywhere.

What all these changes have meant is that parents seem to have all the responsibility for providing and organising their children's activities. Their children's friends probably don't live just down the street, and transport has to be provided for them to go to play with someone. Parents have tended to become entertainment planners and, given that often both parents are working – and busy even when they're not

— the temptation is to leave the children's entertainment to a screen.

We all know that's not the best, but what can you do? Well, some screen-time is fine of course, but try to have it at *set times of the day*, and *for limited periods*. Other things to do are:

- imaginative play with toys;
- creative/artistic activities;
- outdoor play with, say, a ball or a bike;
- reading;
- board games;
- visits to the park or pool; and
- organised sport.

Have a list or chart of things to do, which you or your child can refer to whenever the chant goes up: 'I'm bored.' Be prepared to join in with their play to get them started.

The point is that busy children are happy children, and are much less likely to get into mischief. A little bit of proactive effort on your part will go a long way to prevent misbehaviour occurring in the first place.

CHAPTER 16

Rewards

I'm not a great believer in rewards as a tool for managing children's behaviour, partly because I don't think they are very effective, and partly because I don't think that children should be rewarded for meeting what are just normal expectations for their behaviour and family life.

Star charts of various types have been around for ages, and they can be used *for a short time* to help a child achieve *one specific behavioural target*, but these behavioural targets should not, in my opinion, be for everyday expectations such as making their bed, keeping their room tidy, brushing their teeth, doing their homework or not pummelling their siblings. These are standard requirements, which are simply part of the basic job description for children.

Once you go down the path of rewarding everyday behaviours you'll find that inflation starts to creep in, because the reluctance to perform the particular duty or behaviour is greater than the attractiveness of the reward. So you increase the reward level, and that works better for a while, but then the performance starts to drop off again, so you increase the reward and so on.

Some parents run detailed lists for all the things that need to be done each day, with a pay-off at the end of the week based on the number of ticks achieved. These systems require great diligence and accuracy to run properly, and usually fall over after a while because you can't remember who did what and eventually everyone loses interest.

The very best and most effective rewards for children are not treats and toys, but social rewards from you such as a smile, a hug, a word of thanks or a brief word of recognition or appreciation for a job well done. The power of this kind of response from you far outweighs the transient appeal of any toy or trinket.

Notice that I say 'a brief word' of recognition or appreciation. It has been said many times that praise is important for children, and I have written about this myself, but it seems now that too much emphasis is being placed on it.

It has even been said that children can't have too much praise, but that is clearly not correct. To have any effect, praise must be genuine. If it is gushy, over-the-top or too frequent it becomes devalued and meaningless. There will of course be times when you will want to tell your child that they are the most fantastic kid on the planet, and that's fine occasionally. But the best praise, the praise that really has a positive effect on a child's self-esteem, motivation, and general sense of well-being is *specific* acknowledgement of achievement or appropriate behaviour.

- 'Thanks for picking up your toys, I appreciate it.'
- 'That was an excellent pass you did to the striker. It showed good judgement.'
- 'It's so nice to see you two playing happily together.'

With children who tend to be challenging much of the time, it is easy to get into a pattern of constant negativity and sniping. All children need recognition of good behaviour from time to time, but difficult children in particular need this sort of acknowledgement, partly as an incentive to behave well, partly for the sake of their battered self-image and partly to nurture your relationship with them, which might be rocky at times. For children like this, remind yourself to praise them at least once a day, even if you have to look hard to find something.

If you do want to give material rewards, make them spontaneous and unexpected. 'You guys have been so good all week. Let's go and get an ice-cream.' Surprise rewards have much more impact, and a treat for the whole family is a good idea because it removes any element of rivalry or competition between children if individual rewards are offered. It also strengthens family ties when you have fun together.

CHAPTER 17

Manners and morality

Manners and morality sound like such old-fashioned words and they are not talked about as much these days as they used to be, but they are still of great importance to the well-being and smooth functioning of our society and our families.

Morality is about right and wrong. These are also words that aren't used much in public discussion these days, and seem to have been replaced by inoffensive, neutral words like 'appropriate', 'inappropriate', 'unacceptable', 'okay' and 'not okay'. I guess these terms have taken over because the old religious foundation of Western societies with its moral certainties has largely gone; because moral judgements and opinions are seen today as being relative rather than absolute; and because we tend to live in multi-cultural societies where we don't want to give offence to anyone.

Despite all this, at a basic everyday level everybody

intuitively knows what's right and what's wrong, and there is also a truly remarkable agreement among most people about the basic rules by which our society should live.

So don't feel awkward or hesitant or embarrassed about using 'v-words' – value words – in your home. It's okay to talk about things being 'good', 'bad', 'right' and 'wrong'. Children need to understand and talk about these things, and do indeed have an intuitive understanding of these concepts. Human beings are moral creatures, and the development of your children's moral sense and conscience (another old-fashioned word) is just as important as all the other skills they need to learn and, dare I say it, in the long run probably more important.

So, first of all, be clear about your own values. What do 'right' and 'wrong', 'good' and 'bad' mean to you? Think about how you want these values to be expressed in your family, in the behaviour of your children and in your own behaviour. If possible, give them expression in some of your house rules. You probably won't have many basic and fundamental values, and they won't be complicated. Just things such as being kind, being considerate, helping each other, telling the truth and doing your best.

Having a declared set of family values gives:

- focus to your parenting;
- power and authority to your requests and expectations of your children;
- clarity in your standards and rules;
- cohesion to the family; and
- greater confidence in your parenting.

Manners are basically an expression of the simple principles of consideration and respect for others. They are not about how to hold your knife and fork or all those other arbitrary customs and conventions that were thought so important a few generations ago and which have now fallen away. A person with good manners is one who treats others with respect and courtesy, and tries to put others' needs on a level with their own. We know good manners when we come across them, just as we recognise rudeness.

Good manners are more about *commitment to a principle*

than about specific behaviours or rules such as saying please or thank you. The principle is showing respect and consideration for others. If children are taught the principle, they will gradually learn to do what's required in specific situations.

Having said all that, and coming back to what this book is all about, emphasising good manners in a meaningful, principled way is a very helpful tool in encouraging your children to behave well.

CHAPTER 18

Change the environment

This is a simple one. If your child has a particular behaviour that you have been trying to change without much success, think about how you can change the environment so that the behaviour is less likely to occur.

Good examples are:

- not taking your child to the supermarket if he tends to have a tantrum, or runs away every time you go there;
- not having snacks or sweets in the house if your child tends to help himself; or
- selling the PlayStation if there are constant battles over its use.

This strategy is well worth thinking about if you have a child who frequently misbehaves or is particularly determined and wilful. For recurring problems, think about how you might be able to arrange things to avoid the behaviour occurring in the first place.

....

CHAPTER 19

Be proactive

As a general strategy to avoid children getting into mischief, be proactive.

- Keep them busy.
- Monitor what they're doing.
- When things become quiet, go and see what's happening.

Get involved in their play when you can. Apart from being fun, this is good for building a positive relationship with them, which you can use as 'influence capital' when you need to. (If that sounds manipulative, it's not meant to be. It's just a fact.)

Another helpful tactic is to *intervene early and decisively* when behaviour shows signs of drifting off track. When your parental radar tells you that trouble is brewing:

- Go to where your child is playing.

- Use your physical presence as a steadying influence (good teachers do this in the classroom).

- Use 'the look'. (I don't need to explain that, do I?)

- Ask, 'What are you doing?' or 'What's going to happen if you keep doing that?' (Possible replies to the latter question: 'It'll break.' 'The dog will get upset.' 'We'll end up fighting.')

- Ask, 'So, what should you do?' or 'What's the rule about that?'

- Wait for the appropriate behaviour, and depart.

- Pop around the corner unexpectedly a few minutes later.

Intervening early and defusing a situation is much better than dealing with the mess after the bomb has gone off.

Being a proactive parent takes energy and persistence, but it's worth it.

CHAPTER 20

Your personality

Sorry to say this, but a major factor in whether you are likely to smack your children is your own personality. In my experience, parents who are impatient and quick to anger are more likely to use physical punishment in an impulsive way. Calm, easy-going, patient parents are highly unlikely to be smackers.

It can be hard to admit something like this about ourselves, but if you aren't sure ask someone who will give you an honest and objective answer about whether they think you are inclined to lose it. If they think so, or you know so, you need to engage in some internal dialogue when you find yourself in a situation where you might smack, like so:

'Uh-oh, got to be careful here. I can feel myself starting to get angry. Got to stay cool. Just focus on the behaviour. Ask him what the rule is about. Keep my voice down.

Don't shout. Get a grip. There's no need to smack here. I hate it when I smack. Right, looks like we're sorting it. He's coming round. Situation settled. Well done, you did it.'

If you want to avoid smacking:

- make a firm decision that smacking is not going to be part of your parenting;
- have clear plans and strategies for preventing and managing your children's misbehaviour;
- talk yourself through situations when you might smack (or hand over to your partner at that time); and
- if necessary, give yourself time to calm down then revisit the situation later.

CHAPTER 21

Difficult children

My experience has convinced me that children's personalities are more the product of their genes than their upbringing.

Differences in children's response styles are apparent even in newborns. These recognisable tendencies persist through childhood and into adulthood with a remarkable degree of consistency and continuity. Traits such as adaptability, sociability, being easy-going or intense, being a worrier or a risk-taker, being compliant or combative are, in effect, hard-wired. We accept that children are born with talent in sport, art, music or maths, so why not differences in personality too?

You only have to think about the sometimes dramatic differences in personality among children in the same family to realise that parenting and upbringing have less of an effect than their inborn traits. Our parenting style and the home environment remain largely the same for each child in the family, so why are there such big differences between our children, other than for those related to gender or perhaps birth order? When you think about it, any differences in our parenting style from one child to another are actually *in response to* their different personalities.

A child doesn't arrive in the world like a lump of clay, which can be shaped as we wish. The way I see it, personality is like a prefabricated building. When a child is born, the underlying structure of the personality is already there. Parents get some input into the exterior décor and finishing touches, but the basic framework is pre-assembled.

This topic has been the subject of intense and prolonged academic debate that will no doubt continue to rage for some time, but for me the verdict is in. For children who have not experienced seriously adverse events during their development, such as neglect or abuse, I have no doubt that genes are the most powerful determinant of their personalities.

Now it's all very well if Genetic Lotto has handed you a first-division prize of a sweet-tempered, easy-going, compliant little angel. However, the balls can also come up with a sequence that spells trouble. A small percentage of children, most of them boys, are born with a temperament which, for varying reasons, could be described as difficult.

In my experience, the most common sub-group of these temperamentally difficult boys have a recognisable personality type known as attention deficit hyperactivity disorder or ADHD (sometimes known as ADD). There is ongoing controversy about these children and how best to treat them, but there is no doubt that they exist. ADHD comes in degrees of severity. By far the greatest number of ADHD boys are at the mild end of the spectrum, and are not at all like the ones you see on the TV documentaries. They are active, energetic, impatient, impulsive, excitable, easily bored, annoying, enthusiastic, never satisfied, caring, likeable and generally larger-than-life characters. They are usually outdoor kids who are very good at sport and tend to push the boundaries.

As you can imagine, raising a child like this is much harder than parenting a standard-issue child. The strategies for managing ADHD children, or children with other varieties of difficult temperament, are no different from the ones outlined in this book, but if you feel that your child's behaviour has been persistently and unusually difficult to manage right from the word go, seek a professional assessment. Consulting your family doctor is a good place to start.

If your child is particularly wilful, determined, stubborn and mischievous, and has been like that for as long as you can remember, one practical thing you can do is to stop blaming your parenting. When parents have a chronically difficult child, they often wonder if somehow they are at fault. If challenging children come from a normal, unremarkable home environment and have no history of abuse or neglect, the underlying cause is most likely to be genes, not upbringing. If parents can accept this, they can productively turn the energy wasted in fretting and feeling guilty into better behaviour management.

I tell parents of temperamentally difficult children that what we are trying to achieve is improvement, not transformation. Better management strategies will reduce the number of problems, and perhaps their severity, but cannot change a child's personality, which means that their tendency to be difficult will persist. If you ease off, the problems will return. Also, any improvements will only be maintained if the management strategies are used consistently and continuously. This can be discouraging for parents to hear, but understanding and accepting the reality of the situation can sometimes reduce the constant frustration they feel.

....

CHAPTER 22

Stay cool

With the majority of children things go smoothly most of the time, and any bumps in the road tend to be small ones.

But challenging, chronically difficult children can get your temperature to boiling point, partly because their misbehaviour and non-compliance are more dramatic than the norm, and partly because you seem to be constantly revisiting the same issues. This can be frustrating.

If you have a child like this, the strategies I have outlined will help, but *how* you implement them will affect their success. When a problem arises, try not to be emotional. Try to be businesslike. Focus on the rule at issue. Don't shout and harangue. Don't talk too much. Think iceberg. Be confident that you will resolve this issue in your favour because you have the tools to do so. Be relentless but not angry.

Think of it as role-play. You need to act as if you are completely in charge and control even if you may not feel like that inside. You need to believe that you will win this little battle you are engaged in right now, because with each victory your parental authority and confidence will increase.

This might all sound a bit dramatic and over-the-top, and for most parents it is. But if you have one of the small number of genuinely difficult children, life is full of power struggles. For the sake of your sanity and the overall functioning of the family you must win them, but without the use of physical punishment.

Staying cool will make you appear more authoritative, and will make it more likely that your child will fall into line.

CHAPTER 23

Independence

I think that one of the very important underlying themes in our parenting should be helping our children to become independent in the world.

It is very tempting to try to keep our children close to us and dependent on us, because their love for us and need of us in the early years is very gratifying. We naturally want to nurture them, protect them and simply enjoy them, but one day we have to let them go. When that day comes, we want them to be prepared.

This preparation starts from toddlerhood. Children are programmed to explore their environment, and most of them set about doing this energetically. There is always a balance between allowing them to explore and keeping them safe, but we must keep reminding ourselves that children are hard-wired to find out about the world and to develop new skills and understandings. This urge in them is unstoppable and insatiable. Our role is to guide and monitor their learning experiences so that they continue to grow and develop safely and confidently. Today the sandpit, tomorrow . . . well, who knows, but as far as their ability and enthusiasm will take them.

A major part of the growth to independence is learning how to problem-solve. When you think about it, life is really a very long series of problems and puzzles to deal with. It is by solving these problems and finding our way around obstacles that we grow as people. When your children come up against a problem, before you rush in to rescue them, stand back and let them have a go at it. If they don't want to, encourage them a little. Offer a clue or suggestion. Give a little bit of help if necessary, but also give your children the chance to experience the wonderful satisfaction, the natural high, of working it out for themselves.

The reason I mention this theme in the context of this book is because encouraging your children to independence can also help to prevent behavioural problems. How? Well, if you develop your children's ability to solve problems and help them to become independent and confident young people, with the satisfactions and pride in achievement that this can bring, you are channelling their energies and interests in a positive direction and diverting them from negative behaviours.

Also, energetic and determined children who can be difficult to parent often enjoy new experiences and challenges. Once they have mastered them, there are beneficial effects on their self-esteem and behaviour in general.

CHAPTER 24

Little royals

Over the last few decades there has been a clear trend for women to delay having children, and perhaps to have fewer children as a result. Whatever the reasons for this trend, I have noticed a particular quality in the attitudes of some older parents towards their children.

There is a combination of factors at work with older parents. Firstly, their children are very much planned and anticipated, perhaps conceived with some difficulty, and are therefore very precious. Secondly, people in their thirties do tend to take life a bit more seriously and responsibly than those in their early or mid-twenties. Thirdly, parents who are restrained and thoughtful enough to delay the arrival of children for some time are perhaps more likely to be thoughtful and serious in their approach to parenting, and perhaps to focus more attention on their children when they arrive.

These are not bad things in themselves, but they carry the risk that older parents will dote on their children, worry too much about them, try to be perfect parents or, worse still, try to produce the perfect child.

The main traps that I see for older, conscientious parents, who take their duties very seriously, are that they can:

- turn their children into little princesses or princes whose every wish and whim is catered for;
- treat their children like miniature adults who are involved inappropriately in every aspect of family life;
- worry too much about their children and try to protect them from all hazards and unhappiness; and
- try to fill their children's lives with every opportunity and learning experience possible, particularly in the toddler and preschool years, rather than just letting them play and be children.

All of the above pitfalls have obvious negative consequences for children.

Another group of parents who run the risk of indulging their children are those cases where a child has been very difficult to conceive or there has been a history of previous miscarriages; where a child has survived a very serious illness or accident; or where a parent feels very guilty about separation from their partner. In all these examples, parents can try to make up to the child for the trauma or grief they have suffered by catering to them, giving in to them or indulging them.

Sometimes parents don't realise what they are doing, but we all know what happens when children are indulged. They tend to turn into demanding and controlling little people with an inflated sense of their own worth and importance. They are lovely when things are going their way but diabolical when they're not. Having such power is a bit like a drug that you need more and more of in order to feel good. As a result, little royals are often irritable and discontented for no apparent reason, and trying to placate them just makes things worse.

Being at the beck and call of tiny tyrants can cause great frustration, which sometimes boils over into angry words and smacking. So if you are an older parent, or your child has suffered from illness or trauma, just check that you are not giving more attention, power or status than is healthy for a child to have.

CHAPTER 25

Toddlers and preschoolers

There are no different strategies for managing the behaviour of toddlers and preschoolers, just different emphases. For example, there needs to be more effort put into preventive strategies such as keeping them busy and having good structure and routines in the day.

The inescapable fact about little children is that they are *very time-intensive*. The younger they are the more of your time and attention they need. And if you don't provide these things some other adult has to. Toddlers need constant watching, protecting, helping and involvement from you or some other adult.

Toddlers don't misbehave, they just behave. They want to explore things and touch things and open things and take all the pots out of the cupboard – that's just being a toddler. All you can do is distract and divert them to alternative activities. Smacking is unnecessary, even in situations of physical danger. You won't teach a toddler who can barely speak not to put her finger in a power-point, or pull on the jug cord, by smacking her hand. A firm 'No!' and removing her hand will have just as much, if not more, effect than a smack, because the shock of a smack will probably divert the child's attention from what you are trying to teach her. The best interventions for toddlers are preventive: *monitoring* and *child-proofing the environment.* Keep a close eye on your toddler and arrange things so that she won't do something dangerous, rather than try to teach her to avoid risks she won't understand.

Preschoolers (three- and four-year-olds) are much better able to understand reasons and explanations, but of course still require sensible monitoring in regard to physical dangers. For some particularly active and adventurous preschoolers, child-proofing as well as locks on doors, cupboards and gates may still be needed.

Other strategies I have already mentioned that apply particularly to toddlers and preschoolers are:

- *having good routines* for the basic activities of the day such as getting dressed, mealtimes, bathtime and bedtime, because clear routines are likely to mean greater compliance; and

- *having a structure to the day* with some activities at predictable times. For example, playing with play dough, reading books, listening to music, water play, the sandpit, just pottering in the garden, a little TV and a trip to the park can all be scheduled for different times of the day.

Apart from keeping them busy in a positive way, a predictable structure to the day will help toddlers and preschoolers to feel settled and content.

Being at home with a difficult, demanding toddler or preschooler can be physically and emotionally exhausting, so make sure that you arrange regular relief spells either with your partner or through paid care. If your toddler or preschooler is a particularly active or difficult child, don't feel guilty about using daycare to give yourself some respite and recuperation, or getting some extra sessions if he is already attending preschool. You can't do a good job as a parent if you are exhausted or constantly frustrated, so buying a little peace and quiet makes good sense. Some parents feel guilty about this, particularly if they have made the decision to stay home and be a full-time parent in the early years, but there's no point in running on empty for the sake of an ideal that turns out to be no fun for anyone.

Finally, have realistic expectations for your little ones. One good example that I frequently see is parents telling their three-year-olds not to interrupt an adult conversation, often causing frustration and tears for the child. Little children live in a world of immediacy. When an idea or wish or question comes into their head, they usually want to express it right then and there. I think that trying to teach them patience at this stage is expecting too much. It's much more realistic to excuse yourself to the adult you are talking to, deal with the child's comment or request, then go back to your conversation.

CHAPTER 26

Three strikes

So those are the preventive strategies – in other words, the things you need to do to avoid trouble in the first place. Now we come to the penalties for misbehaviour.

I divide misbehaviour into three categories, based on how you should respond to each of them:

- Trivia, which we *ignore*.
- Moderately serious offences, for which we use the *three strikes* system.
- Serious offences, which require *time-out*. There are three of these offences: *aggression*, *deliberate destruction* and *defiance*.

We have already discussed ignoring in Chapter 14. 'Three strikes' is a system for punishing the misbehaviour of school-age children and young adolescents by withdrawing privileges. It is for misbehaviour that cannot be ignored but is *not serious enough for time-out*. It cannot be used with toddlers or preschoolers because it requires an ability to think about the future consequences of misbehaviour, which is not well-developed in young children.

The system works like this. Firstly, it is important to have made your list of house rules and put them up somewhere. If you involve your school-age children in discussing what the rules should be, this is likely to increase their commitment to the system.

Next, set up a whiteboard with a space to record an X for any breaches of house rules, with enough room for three Xs. Have a separate space for each child.

Underneath this space, write up to about five privileges, one of which will be lost if your child gets *three Xs*. Three strikes and you're out. It is important to write the privileges down so that they can be easily seen, even if your child can't read very well. They act as a visual reminder about the consequences for misbehaviour.

Once your child has got three strikes, you choose which

privilege he will lose, then wipe out the Xs and you're ready to start again.

Choose the privileges carefully. They need to be things/treats/activities that your child really likes; for example, a favourite TV programme, having a friend over, time on the computer or PlayStation, use of the phone, use of his bike or skateboard, or a favourite dessert. The reasons for including several privileges in the list is, firstly, in case your child has a bad patch and gets lots of strikes, and secondly, to enable you to choose a privilege that suits a particular day of the week. A good idea is to include a *wild card*, which is an unspecified privilege. This can be used for unpredicted or irregular events, or just a bright idea you happen to have at the time when you need to select a privilege to be forfeited.

It is very important to note that the privileges are lost for *one day only* or, depending on the privilege, for a weekend at the most. Many parents tend to over-punish in the heat of the moment, which can result in unfair punishments, forgetting how long the punishment is supposed to last or giving up on it because it's such a nuisance. The three-strikes system pretty much guarantees a fair punishment, partly because the duration of the penalty is restricted to one day and partly because the whole system is so transparent.

Here's an example of how it works. One of your house rules is, say, not eating in the lounge. Your child is eating in the lounge. You remind him briefly about the rule. If he responds appropriately, that's fine. If he doesn't you say 'That's a strike', and mark an X on the board. If he then complies, that's the end of it.

The Xs stay on the board until there are three. It doesn't matter how long it takes for your child to accumulate three Xs. It may take five minutes or it may take five days or it may take two weeks. He may lose more than one privilege in a day, or it may take a few days to lose one privilege. Just having an X or two on the board can be enough to keep some children on the right side of the law.

The major strengths of this system are firstly its transparency and fairness, and secondly that it *eliminates the need for big arguments and shouting matches.* Let the whiteboard do the talking: 'You break a rule, you get an X.' There's no need for explanations or lectures or yelling. Just put the X on the board, and let them accumulate. When there are three of them, bang goes a privilege for the day. Leaving the Xs on the board acts like a warning without you having to say anything.

Your child may say he doesn't care about losing something for a day. Ignore this. If you impose these limited penalties consistently, they *will* bite eventually, no matter what he says.

If your child rubs out the strikes in an attempt to destroy the system, don't try to replace them immediately. Just say, 'That's fine, I remember how many strikes there were', and reinstate them that night when he's asleep, or at the next offence.

If on any particular occasion your child stubbornly refuses to comply, even after accumulating three strikes and losing a privilege, send him to time-out (covered in the next chapter). The issue is now one of defiance.

The three-strikes method is not dramatic or powerful, but it represents everything you want your behaviour-management system to be: rule-based, reasonable, fair, transparent, low-key and unavoidable.

CHAPTER 27

Time-out

There never have been many weapons in the parental armoury, but once smacking has been eliminated the bottom-line punishment becomes time-out. Because it is the 'last resort' punishment, it should only be used for the three most serious offences (with one exception I will mention later).

What is time-out?

Time-out is the exclusion of your child from normal family life for a specified period. Time-out sends one very clear message: 'Your behaviour is completely unacceptable. You cannot be part of the family if you behave like that. You are going to be isolated to think about what you have done until I am ready to have you back.' Most children do not like time-out and for most children it is very effective, if used properly.

Apart from being a deterrent to misbehaviour, time-out also has the major advantage that it puts a sudden stop to angry interactions, and gives everyone a chance to calm down.

When should I use time-out?

You should use time-out for the big three offences:

- *aggression*;
- *deliberate destruction*; and
- *defiance*.

Aggression means hitting or hurting of any kind. Deliberate destruction means the wilful damage or defacing of any property. Defiance means refusal to comply with a reasonably important request or directive. There are a few exceptions to the defiance rule, which I will discuss later.

Aggression and destruction earn *immediate* time-out. For defiance, you can give your child a warning that time-out will be the consequence if she doesn't comply.

What is the best place for time-out?

In my opinion the location of time-out is not critical. A bedroom is fine. The key point is *exclusion and isolation*, not location. If you have a spare room, that would also work well. Bathrooms and laundries are risky as they often contain opportunities for further mischief involving taps or toilet rolls, and they also need to be cleared of toxic stuff.

With preschoolers you might be able to use a designated spot such as the bottom of the stairs, a mat in the hallway or a little chair in a corner instead of the bedroom, but this is only likely to work with reasonably compliant children.

How long should time-out be for?

Firstly, don't begin timing *until your child is quiet*. From that point, I think that ten minutes is about right for school-age children, or until *you* have calmed down. Don't worry about the standard rule of a minute of time-out for each year of the child's age. In the end you are the best judge of how long time-out should be for your child, but it needs to be long enough to bite. It has to be a bit painful or it's not a punishment.

It can be helpful to use a timer of some sort, which your child can hear when it goes off. That way there's no need for discussion through the door about how much sentence she has left to serve.

Be prepared that some difficult children may rant and rave for a long time when they arrive in time-out. Remind them *once* that timing doesn't start until they are quiet.

What do I do if my child refuses to go to time-out?

Some very oppositional children may need to be taken to time-out physically. You will probably only have to do this once or twice until they learn that you mean what you say and that you *will* carry them to time-out if you have to. You can give defiant children a choice: they either go to time-out voluntarily for ten minutes or, if you have to take them, it will be for fifteen. Taking a child physically to time-out is not nice. It can create ugly scenes, but you have no choice. Time-out is your last-resort, end-of-the-line punishment. If you don't enforce it, you have effectively given your child the message: 'You are in charge, not me.' However, be aware that using physical force to take a child to time-out is only likely to happen with a small number of very determined and oppositional children.

Should I shut the door?

I think that it's better to shut the door of the time-out room to emphasise the message of exclusion. It also prevents the time-out being undermined by your child being able to stay in contact with you verbally or visually while they are supposed to be in isolation.

For defiant children who won't stay in their room, threaten to lock the door if they come out and carry out your threat if they do. Fitting a lock is a much better option than holding on to the door handle or tying it shut. Give your child the choice: 'If you stay in your room I won't lock the door. If you come out, I will.' You'll probably only need to do this once or twice before she chooses to stay in the room without the door being locked. Holding on to the door while your child tugs on the other side is just teaching her to resist you physically. Tying the door shut in some way is unlikely to be secure, and will therefore be an invitation to your child to see if she can open it by force.

For very difficult children it is virtually certain that you will need to fit a lock to their door if it doesn't already have one. You may also need to fit safety catches to windows if there is a chance your child may try to climb out.

If your child is inclined to throw things around in time-out, remove breakables from the room beforehand. Time-out needs to be *safe* and *secure*, so that you can leave your child there for the duration of their sentence without worrying. If she trashes the room, she needs to tidy it up to a reasonable degree before she comes out. Warn your child that anything broken in a tantrum will not be replaced.

What should I do when the time is up?

When time is up, open the door and say, 'You can come out now.' If your child chooses not to, that's fine, just leave her to it. If she's found something to play with in the meantime, that's fine too. The purpose of time-out has still been served. It goes against the grain for some parents that their child ends up playing in their room during what is meant to be a punishment, but remember that the point of time-out is exclusion and isolation from family life. Your child may play the 'I don't care' game with you, but that is just a tactic.

Avoid lectures or sermons after time-out. Lectures are likely just to re-ignite things and are unlikely to be listened to anyway. Briefly ask your child why she was sent to time-out, and what she will do next time that situation arises. If there needs to be an apology to someone that's fine, but don't expect it to be heart-felt. If your child was sent to time-out for defiance, she is now given another chance to comply. If she doesn't, it's another dose.

I don't recommend giving hugs after time-out, because it undermines the whole point of the exercise and sends a very confusing message about what time-out is for.

From what age can you use time-out?

Depending on a child's maturity and language skills, time-out can be used from about the age of two-and-a-half. Try using a designated spot for preschoolers, but the feisty ones may need to go to their room.

A fourth reason for using time-out

I said at the beginning of this chapter that there are three behaviours that deserve time-out, namely aggression, deliberate destruction and defiance (think ADD). However, a fourth situation that can justify using time-out is when you have had it up to here. Maybe your child has been in a particularly niggly and combative mood all afternoon, and you have just had enough. Send her to her room and leave her there until you feel you are ready to see her again. When she does come out, it's probably a good idea to start afresh by suggesting a mutually enjoyable activity to get things back on the tar-seal.

Generally speaking, if things have degenerated into chaos and anarchy, the best way to restore order is with a liberal dose of time-out.

Final points

As with all behavioural strategies, explain to your child exactly how the time-out system works. If everyone is clear about the procedure it is likely to work better.

Never lock your child outside the house for time-out, because you then have absolutely no control about where they go or what they get up to. Parents usually resort to this option with very difficult children, but such children often use it as an opportunity for great mischief.

Lastly, there are two areas of defiant behaviour where I don't think you should use time-out. One is eating, and the other is getting ready for preschool or school. I discuss these situations in the next chapter.

CHAPTER 28

Examples

Here are some examples of common behavioural problems and my suggestions for how to handle them.

Eating

Mealtimes can be a cause of much stress in some families. This is because some children, usually boys, are very fussy eaters, and getting children to eat a healthy diet is something that parents tend to take seriously. The clash between these two positions can turn just about every mealtime into a frustrating and unpleasant battle.

My suggestion is to go with the flow. You cannot change the taste buds of a fussy eater. You also cannot force them to eat. So give them what they *will* eat (provided that it's not totally unhealthy of course) with tiny side portions of what you would *like* them to eat.

Usually when you look at what fussy eaters are taking

in over the course of the day, they are actually getting a reasonable range of nutrients. If you are worried that they are not, you should check with your doctor, maybe use a dietary supplement and/or sneakily add healthy ingredients to the things they do eat.

Big showdowns are a waste of time with chronically fussy eaters. Don't save uneaten food for presentation at the next meal. Don't send them to time-out even though they are technically being defiant. Give them a set time to finish a meal then, when time's up, bin what's left over or give it to the dog. Be very strict about not grazing between meals or set snack-times.

Bedtime

Putting children to bed can be one of the nicest times we spend with them during the day, but in some families it can be a battle. Most children happily hop into bed for stories and cuddles but a small percentage actively resist it. They don't want to go to bed and they don't want to go to sleep. They will do everything they can to prolong and sabotage the process.

These children need firm treatment. Firstly, have a clear bedtime routine and a definite bedtime. Have a set, non-negotiable number of stories that will be read. When the routine has reached the goodnight-kiss stage, depart and turn out the light. If your child calls out, tell him to go back to sleep. If he keeps calling out, do not respond. If he comes out of the room, take him back with minimal comment.

Now at this point you have two choices. If your child keeps coming out, you can do the yo-yo routine of back-and-forth, back-and-forth until he gives up. Or you can get the whole business over with by saying that if he comes out again you will lock his door. Then if he comes out again you lock the door. There will probably be loud wails and entreaties, which may go on for a long time. Do not respond to these. Eventually your child will go to sleep. He may go to sleep on the floor by the door. If he does, you can go in later and put him to bed. The next night, repeat the process. For most children about three nights will do it. It will not cause them psychological harm. Those are the two options: the choice is yours.

Some children actually find it hard to go to sleep. Their biological clocks seem to be set an hour or two later than you would expect for their age. If this is the reason your child resists going to bed, it can be a sensible option to allow him to read or play quietly in his room until he is ready to go to sleep, provided that he doesn't come out.

Some children want to come into your bed during the night. If you don't mind it, that's over to you. If you don't like it, the only real solution is to take your child back to his own room as soon as you are aware that he's in your bed. Repeat the process once, then warn him that you will lock his door if he comes out again. You can try the yo-yo system if you want, but it is hard to do at 2 a.m.

Problems away from home

Let's say you have things pretty well sorted at home, but your child can sometimes be difficult when you're out shopping or at a friend's place. Here's the drill. Before you arrive at a potential trouble spot, remind your child about what he did last time. Tell him that if the same thing happens again, he will have time-out in the car or somewhere else suitable (plan A). If he then carries on misbehaving, you will be going home (plan B). If you are visiting friends or relatives, tell them that this may happen. Then carry through with your threats. Time-out in your car or in an unfamiliar venue can be awkward, but give it a go. If it's not working, go straight to plan B.

Don't be embarrassed or hesitant about speaking firmly to your child in public if his behaviour is drifting. You need to show him that he doesn't have the upper hand just because you are away from home. Be prepared to abandon an outing if there is an incident of serious misbehaviour, *with time-out to follow at home.*

Sibling conflict

Almost all siblings will squabble from time to time. My suggestion is to leave them to sort it out themselves until it either becomes a full-on fight or you are sick of the bickering. At that stage, put them both into time-out. Don't waste your time trying to find out who started it. If you punish them both, then they will both be motivated to get along with each other, or at least to keep their disagreements quiet. Either outcome is acceptable.

Getting ready for school

Getting ready for school can be stressful if you have one of those children who are easily distracted or drift off to play rather than brush their teeth. As a first step, try having a chart with a list of the main things that have to be done, and the times they have to be done by. Call out the time periodically as a prompt.

This probably won't do the job for the hard cases so, particularly for younger children, I often suggest dedicating about fifteen minutes to being physically present and focused as your child gets ready. Stand by, point to the list, hand over the socks, put the toothpaste on the toothbrush, and generally keep the process moving along. This is a better option than doing things by remote control and intermittent yelling over the course of an hour, with the job still not done at the end of it.

With older children, tell them what time you will be waiting in the car, then leave them to organise themselves. Toot the horn if necessary. If they walk or catch a bus, tell them what time they need to be out of the house then leave them to it. Tell them that if they are late they will need to explain why to their teacher, and that you won't be writing a note. Emphasise the consequences for them if they are not ready on time. Don't use time-out for non-compliance with getting ready, because that just slows everything down even further.

CHAPTER 29

Summary

So, there you have it. The full story on what you need to do to avoid smacking. The key points I have made in this book are as follows:

- I have never met a parent who wants to smack their children.
- Parents invariably regret smacking.
- My experience has shown me clearly that the great majority of children do not need to be smacked.
- For a small percentage of genuinely difficult children, it may look like a smack is needed to keep them in line, but for these children it doesn't really work.
- Children can be well-behaved almost all the time without the need for smacking.

- Effective parenting strategies can greatly reduce the number of situations where you might be tempted to smack.
- Effective parenting strategies used on an everyday basis are a much better option for everyone in the family than relying on smacking.
- There is no doubt that good parenting takes effort, practice and perseverance, while smacking is a quick and easy response to bad behaviour, but is there really any doubt about which way you would prefer to go?

Prevention of problem behaviour is very important in avoiding the use of smacking. Prevention takes effort, patience and perseverance, but it will make you a more effective parent. The key factors in preventing misbehaviour are to:

- Spend time with your children and keep them busy.
- Act with confidence.

- Be in charge.
- Be clear and explicit about your personal values and about the sort of people that you want your children to become.
- Have clear house rules that reflect your family values.
- Have good routines for the basic activities of the day.
- Don't ask ten times. Ask once, give a reminder, then act.
- Mean what you say.
- Avoid lengthy sermons, lectures and post-mortems.
- Don't negotiate, bribe, cajole or bargain.
- Don't *invite* children to do the basic activities of daily living – *tell* them.
- When you need to intervene because of misbehaviour, intervene early and decisively.
- With chronic problems, see how you can change the environment to prevent the problem occurring in the first place.

- Ignore minor problems, but be consistent in what you ignore.

Despite all your preventive efforts, there will be times when you will need to impose a punishment on your children. The two major punishments in your armoury are loss of privileges and time-out. They are part of the four-stage system for dealing with misbehaviour, which is:

1 **Prevention** through effective parenting.
2 **Ignoring** minor misbehaviour.
3 **Three strikes**, which is a structured method of losing privileges for breaking house rules.
4 **Time-out** for the most serious offences.

Personality is an issue in smacking, both your own and your child's. In my experience hot-headed parents are more likely to smack. This is something worth reflecting on, and being aware of when you become annoyed with your children.

Your child may be one of the small percentage who are particularly difficult to manage because of their temperament.

The strategies in this book will help you to manage him more effectively, but if you still feel you are struggling you should seek professional guidance.